AF225085

WELLING UP

Palewell Press Anthology

WELLING UP

Welling Up – Palewell Press Anthology

First edition 2019 from Palewell Press,
www.palewellpress.co.uk

Printed and bound in the UK

ISBN 978-1-911587-26-2

All Rights Reserved. Copyright © 2019. No part of this publication may be reproduced or transmitted in any form or by any means, without permission in writing from the authors. The right of the various authors to be identified as the author of this work has been asserted by them in accordance with the Copyright, Designs and Patents Act 1988

The cover design is Copyright © 2019 Camilla Reeve

The cover photograph, downloaded from Shutterstock.com, was taken by http://www.shutterstock.com/g/Marton+Kallai

A CIP catalogue record for this title is available from the British Library.

ACKNOWLEDGEMENTS

"Water from the Well" was published initially in Wey Poets' anthology *Ripples,* 2016.

"Blackbird Love" first appeared in *The Grain of my Life* by Muir Hunter (pb Tears in the Fence 1997).

"Dawn" and "Storm Warning" appeared in *Metamorphosis* by Gillian Petrie (pb Palewell Press 2018).

"The Small Cabin" by Jack Houston appeared in *Brittle Star.*

"Cumbria" and "Shimmer" by Christie Dickason appeared in *The Balancing Dance* (pb Ollerton Press 2006).

"English Lessons" by Tim Waller was commended in the Barnet competition.

"From Part IV 'for Yolick and all migrating birds' in the Second Episode," and "Part III from The Fourth Episode," are extracts from *The Episodes, A Secret History of the Cold War* by David Kuhrt 2008.

Dedication

This anthology is dedicated to the Palewell Press poets who, sadly, are no longer with us – Derek Summers and Frances White – and to those authors prevented by circumstance from joining us at this year's Mini Book Festival.

CONTENTS

FOREWORD

Welling Up is the first anthology composed of writing submitted to Palewell Press, with selection based on our core values of justice, equality and sustainability. I'm sometimes asked why we focus on these values.

Modern society needs a legal system whose laws define and echo what its citizens believe to be fair and acceptable behaviour. Though laws change over time, their existence provides stability to life on any given day. But justice is usually out in front of the laws of a particular time, pulling the sledge as it were, towing the legal system into closer alignment with changed public opinion.

My father was a barrister and volunteered as an Amnesty Observer at trials of prisoners of conscience, including some where prisoners had been tortured. He believed passionately in the concept of Natural Justice, and that there were certain acts or situations which every human would agree were unjust. Yet we know ideas constantly evolve. What seems fair to most people at a particular time will alter once they realise the justifiable needs of certain groups or individuals are not being met.

While laws may change, equality is essential too—for everyone, not only those in elite groups or unionised employment, to be treated equally under the law, their rights respected with state-subsidised representation in court where necessary, and their other needs met too, including health, safe housing, social care, education, and freedom of movement, belief and cultural expression.

At few moments in human history has any society had enough resources and a sufficiently developed sense of fairness so that none of its members felt excluded or short-changed. But now, due to climate change, the natural world's resources on which our safety and happiness depend are more threatened than ever. To have any hope of delivering justice and equality to the world's citizens, including refugees and displaced people, and also protection to other, increasingly endangered, species, we need to collaborate towards environmental sustainability.

I'm delighted that *Welling Up* brings together such a strong set of voices, all with views urgently needing to be heard; from writers at the start of their poetry journey through to those who already have collections published. As with any anthology, many different viewpoints are represented, not all of which are shared by the editor. But I want to thank each of the writers for their unique and moving contributions on our linked themes.

Camilla Reeve, August 2019

Lost Girls

So many societies, contemporary as well as historical, have regarded women as being of less value than men. Now the world's peoples are re-evaluating the rights, roles and importance of women, those who have witnessed or experienced gender-based oppression feel impelled to share their stories.

Water from the Well – Belinda Singleton

If his culture had been otherwise,
if Abdul had been called another –
such as Aquarius – even then, despite
the naming of need, would he have
stooped in unblinking African sun
to lower a pitcher at the well,

the only well within village reach?
Would he have stooped again to lift
the silver unwavering on to his head,
treasuring it home barefoot but sure?
No, only his sister is stooping here.
She carried an empty pitcher to class,

and now it is only his sister who
stoops at the well near the school,
drawing no lesson from the indivisible
uncultured names of the water as she
stoops again and sways upright,
like her mother and older sisters

who'd had no classes to go to,
like her aunts, great-aunts, grandmother,
like generations lost in a female telling.
Will her daughters know life bearing water
or, by the time that water falls freely,
will all their names have been swallowed?

Unmorality – Veronica Oyoko

I refuse to be paralysed by fear
Your unmoral outrage won't stop me from my rebellion
My compassion may seem as a self-destructive mechanism
but comforting as I may sketch my own undoing.
I control it, I will control all of it.

I will be here to enjoy their liberation, my liberation
and my body will contribute to its embodiment

I refuse to accept the silence of others to be absolute
Is seeking justice a sin?
because I won't hesitate to come forward as a sinner

My nights are just days in extension
Insomnia has become a reality
as my demons see this as an opportunity for a reunion
They carry your smell

Justice has a price
one I must afford
I waited for time to heal my wounds,
but instead they got bigger and bigger overtime

I will be here to enjoy their liberation, my liberation
and my body will contribute to its embodiment

I know how
I will pay for it
and it will be more than accountability
something that every system seems to lack these days
I will give resistance a new meaning
when the day comes
to pay

From a Black Mother – Irma Upex-Huggins

Maybe if you look, close
thru mi catatonic eyes
you might find me remembering
England take babies from mothers
monitor madness
set services that carry a graveyard smell.

These 'delusions of grandeur' in my world
take me round the palaces of mi mind, where
I am laughing as I hold a conch shell to mi ear
I communicate with voices, dance with visions
laugh on shores of sun-ripe skins in petticoats
I frolic in the innocence of my panty cover-up
waist high, hungry for the caress of each wave
sink into the embrace to hide my naked flirting.

black flesh how flat and heavy you feel now
your nose was once proud and uppity your walk
into that burgeoning seduction of your charms
a challenge to innocence
or disobedience to the code
I sigh the sadness of children
pulled from you one by one before weaning time.

I just cool out now and laughing how I cock
a nosy childhood like a precocious hibiscus
to church tongues spreading scandal by bible verse
listen to the smash of innocence on malicious rocks.
Scents of yesterday, honeysuckle-evenings faded
except inside a laughing underneath a watery sun
beyond the salvation of church and state
I choose to sit with ghosts remembering
the yellow sun cooling to a yellow moon
gods higher than mental health laws

restore me to beautiful names
I am free to ride new winds that
soar above taming hypocrisy of prayers
detentions that scorch, shrivel identities
winds sweeping the good of church,
the laws and language of catatonic eyes.

From Veins of Our Grandmother – Irma Upex-Huggins

Letter to a fickle camera

A click and the images you hold are gone
Prey to unforgiving digital thorns
There is no death says that illusion
Alas your betrayal is a fast-changing tide

I am swept out in desolation
Clinging to the past
Reaching for the storyteller *
The ghost-maker of starless nights
Born from imaginations of her tongue
I find night-time ghosts telling stories
Fearful ones who cared for no moon
Pursuing me in daytime punishing sun
I hold on to colours of the Caribbean
Sounds as moments alive in my head
The memories dancing
I am the gift of that childhood

I find the smell of made up stories
In wrappings that sweeten a hard memory
I find her, cutlass in hand, chopping wood
To make a good bed of fire
She will then count days by smoke signals
To open the kiln on time: not late, not early
Reap the burned wood now turned to coal
By her standards, reached not by book or school

I watch her fan the coal-pot, so smoke
Swing and swirl and catch the years
A majestic pulsating from the sacred fire
We eat rice and salt fish, cooked to perfection

Our memories tumble down laughing
In our time come from good water
We have been to the underground

I love her now we are old and fat
My hair a long grey tangle of ropes
That wind us unseparated to the root
We flow from the veins of our grandmother
Go barefoot in the dirt
We, inheritors of a woman, un-tamed.

*Footnote: *Mavis Samuel, my beloved cousin was orphaned by the age of 5. She experienced a 'rough' life, had no formal education but had a "rich" imagination and a natural bond with the soil.*

The Obey Doll – Sunita Thind

This strangulation you impose upon me father.
Culturally choking me with a *chuni* mother.
Curry the favour of both sides? British and Asian?
                 Woman and wife? Daughter and Sikh?
Am I a paraplegic to this so called chastity I must maintain?
Who shall dictate the terms and conditions of my life?
My body is my cultural gallery.
My mind is my religious exhibition.
Who shall toll my virginal bell?
Who is thieving my liberation? My womanly rights.
Sikhism? Family? Husband? Society?
What is this gender imbalance?
Shackled to these repressed *churia?*
Is it gilded to be a Sikh? A Sikh woman? A woman?
I follow my own cultural corridor!
I am my own deity.
Imprinted on my forehead is my slavery, my dowry
             by exquisite henna-mendhi.
Threading the oppressed and stitching me with
            admonished words.
I am not the obey doll.

Dead House – Sunita Thind

This house is expired-blood blind.
A fortification of chattering stone.
Rubble-crying.
The pelvis of the house is moaning.
Once a terrain of ingenuity.
Its blood is bone white.
Ectoplasm in deadened walls.
This viscous substance leaving its skeleton.
Rubbing its brick tongue together.
Wishing for resurrection of its splintered wood.
Its feuding doorways crackle.
Landscape now ignorant.
No scrubbed floors familiar with dust.
No new quench of paint or lustre of ornament.
Coffin roofs littered with dead owners.
Wallowing is the soot and the ghost.
Blood brimming.
Water is fouled in these windless rooms.

The Lost Girls of Brockhall – Tina Morris

To feel loved
if only for a moment,
other times raped
but the young girls
in their frail cotton dresses and clogs
were deemed too weak of spirit or mind
to keep themselves safe in a wicked world
and, ripe with babies,
were removed from society
into an Institution for Mental Defectives.
The babies were wrenched away for adoption at birth
and the girls, grieving and howling,
put to work in the laundry or scrubbing floors.

Young girls imprisoned there
with mad women and sad women
and women turned beastly through anger.

The world revolved without them
with no contact or news of family.
The air vibrated
with the silent wailing of loss.
Nothing to mark their place on the earth
except nameless children growing in the anguish
of having been given away.

So many years of life with nothing to celebrate
except birth names marked in scratchy writing
in the Parish Registers…
…names acknowledging their admittance
to the 'Inebriate Women's Reformatory'
…and entries in a different hand
recording their death in the Hospital ledger
fifty or more years later.

Nobody will ever release the girls
from the never-ending pain.
No Enquiry will find them innocent.
And no-one will even remember them.
Their lives were one long rape
and their single moment of feeling loved
was simply that…
a moment

Footnote: *Brockhall Hospital, in the Ribble Valley, Lancashire, was claimed to be one of Europe's largest mental institutions. It was built in 1904 as an Inebriate Women's Reformatory, later becoming a hospital for people with learning disabilities.*

A World Gone Mad

Humans and other live creatures differ from non-organic systems since our reactions to destructive stress, whether stored as memory or scars, are irreversible. Even helped by counsellors, famine relief agencies or political reformers, we can only move on from where we find ourselves, never back. In order for those who have suffered to be able to move on, they need others to acknowledge what has happened to them.

I was never beaten as a child – Max Fishel

I was never beaten as a child
maybe that was because my father
wasn't there most of the time
away four nights, in for three
just my mum and me
not speaking much at all
passing each other in the kitchen
or the hall
the front room full of books
about the holocaust
and concentration camps of course
naked skeletons in a pit
were the companions I grew up with

she told me to be careful
every time I left the house
the Nazis were out there,
in Liverpool 17,
Smithdown Road leading to the gas chambers
at the Pier Head
the number 5 bus my own kindertransport
to hell
in her mind

the man and woman I called my parents
fed and clothed me well enough
he
made the money
she
cleaned the house
I
did my homework
they
said I was a Jew,
assumed I was a Jew
as far as they knew

Man Runs For Train – Pete Murry

There's someone running for a train.
As the train moves off down the track
Someone doesn't stop,
Because he's come so far,
He's gotta catch the train,
There's no turning back.
And inside, the passengers sit back,
As the train gathers speed, rolling right on track,
Now they know they're safe on the train,
It should be in on time.
In comfortable seats they start to relax.
Someone makes a jump,
A desperate dive,
He might not get inside,
But, at least he'll get on board,
If he can hang on,
As it rolls down the track.
If he can find a handle.
Or something to grip,
With hands or feet or arms,
And fight off the cramp,
Then the train will take him too,
Then the train will take him far,
Then the train will make him safe,
Then the train will make him rich,
Or stop him being poor.
If he doesn't fall away,
As the train rolls away,
So that he rolls away as he falls onto the track.

And if he doesn't die right there,
As the passengers relax.
If he falls off the train,
And he doesn't break his back,
He'll get back up again,
Run for another train
Unless he changes the plan,
And adopts a different strategy,
In regard to the logistics
Of being a refugee.
He could float on a tyre
Or stowaway on a ship,
He could slip past a perimeter,
And get into the airport,
Or pretend to be cargo,
In the back of a van.
He could even buy permits,
if he could find some money,
And sit back in the train,
As it rolls down the track,
Whilst someone else does the running,
Because there'll always be someone,
Running for the train,
Towards a dream before them,
With a nightmare at their back.

Footnote from Pete Murry*: I make no claim to powers of prophecy, I wasn't the only one to see it, but I wrote this in about 2001, how tragic and shameful that nothing has changed.*

The Gaits That Lag Us – Sahr Nouwah

Mastered and schooled in lies,
We humbly admired them showdown,
Telling us lies, even when we know the truth,
In their scornful and mournful lies, they strive like bees.

I am thunderstruck,
That a nation built with blood and iron,
Well thought by those who founded it,
Will even crop such progenies.

Like they tell us, nothing is impossible,
But these sons and daughters have proven impossible,
Their bellies sing their riches,
Their only contribution is dearly carried in their graves.

What a nation, what a people,
So religious, so corrupt,
So pure, so dark in dealings,
Yet preached us an open society.

Life, so funny, so calling to us all,
As man firmly entrenched his vigor in Sleaze,
They are our complexities,
The world dawdles forever.

They prick us,
Even their own,
And they humbly boast being wise and learned,
Their own devil smiles at them.

Who will come to our rescue,
To rescue us from our own,
The cornerstones we positioned,
Now wolf us with remedy seen from vistas.

Is there hope for a rebirth?
Surely, no doubt if there is any,
The world well doomed without hope,
Hatch netted and praised by the enemy.

From the wasteland, stressful souls sing the arrival of day,
By the foil of their deeds, they fall forever,
Good Souls now arrive sturdier,
Human Horror, melting in the sands forever.
At the welcome party,
Crowd smile inimitably,
The new heroes are steadier,
No more shall this nation ever fall.

Peace - My Missing Piece – Sahr Nouwah

Man, left to his wisdom,
Selfish ends felt deep with woes,
The whole of the whole is doomed,
With trumpet sounding soundless sounds.

For the golden, hope do arrive,
For the Helpless, it's a lost gain,
As women and children perish,
In vanity and vanquish.

Men of wisdom wandering and wondering,
For all hopes remained doomed,
Where are you,
We seek you fervently.

Others detest you for own gains,
Wealth, they claimed to amaze,
Humanity remains a cost to pay,
Women, children, elderly, all left to rot.

As vanity upon vanity looms,
Lost to anger, strife and pain,
Endlessly, they endure the pains of war and poverty,
Injustice is justified by the privileged,
The deprived hoping to embrace you.

Peace, oh Peace!
The earth yearns for you,
The world searches endlessly,
With keenness and kindness
Our voice, less heard beyond the mountains.
Peace, oh peace,
Your coiled love embraces all,
As your old spots are well known,
As your freedom is well freely offered.

Man, when returns to his senses,
As a prodigal returned to his father,
Shall you dwell in us and on us,
Lashing our pains away forever.

In the eclipse of the dying day,
Man, smilingly bows to welcome you,
Even children just born smile,
For your presence is felt by all,
As we all embrace Peace at last.

No Ordinary Child – Jenny Messer

He sits so small on an over-sized chair
as if he's just jumped from the pages
of Alice in Wonderland.

This is no ordinary child
sitting at a Tea Party.
There are grazes and blood on his face.

Where is his 10-year-old brother, Ali?
He doesn't know yet but Ali lies buried
under the rubble of their home.

Five-year-old Omran
can only sit in the ambulance
looking at a world gone mad.

Aleppo August 2016

The Craiglockheart Patient – George Wright

He stated he was finished with the war
While writing a soldier's declaration.
He'd lost the point of what it was for;
Neither self-defence nor liberation.

His government, he knew, could stop the guns,
Yet encouraged their continuation.
They went to their churches, prayed for their sons,
Ensuring they were safe from damnation.

What the soldier had seen at the front
Caused him pain beyond all belief,
His many dead friends bore the brunt.
No armistice would bring them relief.

Then they labelled him with "shell-shock,"
In preference to having him shot.

Footnote: *In 1917 Siegfried Sassoon was sent by a Medical Board to Craiglockhart Hospital, near Edinburgh, after an excoriating letter he had written about the ethics of the First World War had been read out in Parliament.*

Lines of Longitude – Margaret Whittock

i. Fortaleza de Sagres, Portugal

Out on the edge of Europe the great fort squats,
brooding in the heat.
Here, before the earth moved and the wave fell,
Vasco da Gama paced and plotted charts.
Sailing away on the São Gabriel,
seeking routes to undiscovered parts.
Now, between its thick stone walls,
wildflowers bloom like stars,
Grey lilies tremble in the breeze,
ghostly ladies waiting on a wild Atlantic shore.

ii. Rosroe, Ireland

Out on the edge of Europe a tiny hamlet lies;
the last pool of darkness in the world.
Here the philosopher sits alone,
head in hands, stares at the blank page:
Tractatus Logico-Philosophicus: brilliant words caged.
He glances up toward the stars,
white flowers strewn across the sky.
Each a bright memorial to those who left these shores,
crawling onto famine ships:
backbroken, heartbroken, where the wild Atlantic roars.

iii. New York

Where the wild Atlantic roars,
new cities rose up from mosquito-ridden shores.
Raised high by the children of famine victims
who'd struggled and survived,
people who formed a continent
where new forms of justice thrived.
And with them on their journey,
descendants of another diaspora, men and women,
bound hand to hand, stolen away from pillaged lands.
Da Gama's shameful legacy; Ireland's tragic history.

And away, away, on the edge of Europe, stars glimmer,
the white flowers shiver.

'I Only Know What I Believe.' – Mike Harwood

*From Tony Blair's speech at the Labour Party
Conference, September 2004*

I'm acting on my instincts
with George Bush on my sleeve,
our information is distinct,
I only know what I believe.

There were no weapons of mass destruction,
but you gave them shock and awe;
the threats exaggerated
to start a bogus war.

Those weapons will destroy us,
we think that they are there,
a real and threatening danger,
the war we all must share.

The crucible is melting,
armed Militia running by
with mortar bombs and rockets
that brighten up the sky.

All things bright and beautiful,
Iraq's a better place,
All our strategies for peace,
will make the country safe.

Each empty pile of sandals,
each jagged blast the cost,
the fruits of your legacy?
Six hundred thousand lost.

The power man's in his coterie,
young soldiers at the gate,
bless all those who serve with him:
he ordered their estate.

How great will be our victory,
George wears me on his sleeve:
judgements aren't the same as facts,
I only know what I believe.

Belsen – Jane Sherwin

Birds do not live around Belsen;
even now, 73 years later, they are absent,
the trees and hedgerows are all silent,
Pre-warned by the same inherent instinct
that takes them winging safely over half the globe
year after year.

As they would flee a tsunami
they fled the coming Holocaust
of malice, brutality and suffering.
And for them, as for many human survivors,
the deep wounds of that trauma
linger.

Perhaps, viewed from space,
a loathley black swastika
still marks the map.

Are there birds singing
in the Rohingya Delta?

REMEMBERED FACES

Many of Palewell Press's publications concern broad sweeps of social history, like the struggles of our world's 65,000,000 displaced people. This section acknowledges those moments we've all encountered when what happens to, or because of, just one person or a few of them, outweighs the bigger picture.

Where are you? – Tina Morris

Are you in there,
buried under heaps of unregulated turmoil?
The You, that used to be,
has become grumpy,
unkempt and inarticulate.

We wait for you to pop up
shouting "only kidding!"
but even your sense of fun
has been bypassed
by endless repetitive questions.

Are lights flicking out
one by one
as synapses fizzle into stray ends,
memories of who we were together
festering into nothing?

And you don't even hear
the sound of my heart breaking
as the lights go out.

Patience – Martin Brummitt

I waited and waited
And gave him lots of space.
I still waited
Later, I saw him outside, but only nodded to him
And still gave him his space.
Later still, he started saying Hello to me.
I responded by talking to him.
We talked about his favourite football team
Chelsea.
And then, when he wasn't busy
We played fox and geese.

The Stones of Venice – Margaret Whittock

Standing on this sun-warmed bridge, I drift across the years,
through Canaletto skies, egg-shell blue above my head.
Beneath my roving feet, flashy gondolas compete between
                                               the marble domes.
Blinking tears away I stare, undone by Ruskin's gorgeous
                                                 Stones.
Why do I feel such sadness now? Thinking of my father,
                                             loving, kind,
who worked hard for so little, yet didn't end up bitter.
Last of a line of stonemasons: men though hardened, gritty,
line up beside me now, captivated by this startling city.

Back then, there were no ships or planes for us,
just trains to the seaside in summer months.
On the platform, waiting: a little girl with plaits;
bucket and spade in hand, hugging dreams of other lands.
Sheltered by the sea wall my mother dried my sandy toes.
Where will these feet go, she wondered?
If only she had known.

On Ponto Del Academia two worlds collide,
I weep for the pity of it all: my parents' little lives;
for the endless, needless compromise;
my long goodbyes.

Gallipoli, We Didn't Know You – Jenny Messer

Armistice Day again,
so many poppies and
lives gone.
A century since
a Grandfather I didn't know
perished.
In the water, on land, how?
A name on a cross
looking out over the Dardanelles.
What could your life have been
how different for your son,
my father,
barely two years old.

Gallipoli, we didn't know you.

A place, a name on a map.
All those young lives lost.
Mothers losing husbands,
then sons in another country,
to another World War.

My tears flow
like poppies falling
over too many battlefields.

Descent – Kathleen Cornelia

I remember a day
in Fortnum and Mason
when we giggled

The waitress's starched uniform
holding her like a prisoner
while we ate crusty scones

Swims in Raquette lake
a loon's mournful wail
piercing daybreak

Treking up Madeloc
Spain waiting below
a village café our reward

Evening discussions
Shakespeare, Joyce
and dreadful Cameron

Our life not yet spent
Expectant, exciting
as champagne popping

Mysterious falls
ambulances and hospitals
a diagnosis

An unspoken plummet
heels digging in
against time.

Dawn – Gillian Petrie

A flutter breaks the surface of our sleep.
Fear is tangible. He stoops, and with his
certain tenderness, he cups the bird —
a marten living underneath our eaves —
one hand across the breast, the other
spanning agitated wings. He frees
the wanderer, which hovers in the air,
then finds a gust and switches on to power.

A blackbird flutes a prelude and the chorus
catch the fugue from tree to tree.
Lying fesse-wise on our feather bed,
we listen to the serenade. I touch
the hand so ready to engage, to show
how love should be and how to let it go.

The Small Cabin – Jack Houston

imagine being the person who has to deliver the fuel

the smell of the petroleum in your hair on your hands

stopping at a roadside café for a hot tea and a burger

fried on a griddle and served in a freshly toasted bun

the rumble of the engine below your bum as it strains

to pull that articulated weight that fat and silver cigar

accelerating up every three-lane blacktop's slow-lane

gently leaning into every corner but unable to u-turn

as there's never room for driving through the driving

rains and hails and sometime snows nothing to stop

you getting to where you have to go the sun hot and

reflected in your right wing infusing the atmosphere

making the small cab you sit in uncomfortably warm

And then he mentioned he was currently 'sleeping outside' – Jack Houston

"In an emergency, buyers have no freedom. The purchase of necessities like safe lodging are forced."— Charlie Crist, Governor of Florida (Rep.)

Outside, as if in an open boat, each warm current
    lapping at the gunwales, sails
        tucked fast to the boom.

Outside, in the crackling air of the city,
    breathing the beneficent smog of our industries,
        of many more than a million cars.

Outside, where it's cool, wrapped up
    in the thick coat, the boots, the sleeping bag;
        like an infant, swaddled.

Outside and free to awake when he wants to,
    to stretch and stand up and move onward
        not held by house or home.

Outside, and every bright star of the galaxy
    a pinprick of paradise
        welcoming him to the night.

Diaspora – Patric Cunnane

If they spoke Irish they kept it quiet
Apart from amadaun, eejit or codding

They left their language behind
Along with family and farms

Bred sons and daughters
To continue the chain

New lands offered a cool welcome

They left their language
Transported music and lyrics
Nurtured history and myths

Mastered unfamiliar idioms
Prone to the shock of the strange

Sailing onwards until morning came
The past becalmed, new earth claimed

It is the Sound – Frank McMahon

of a child abandoned on a hillside
of a man's tears falling across a rock
of a seabird caught in a trough of oil
of a whale lost amongst the throb of engines
of a mother pleading for the life of her child

It is a sound
drawn from wet, wind-hammered fells
drawn from the curlew's piping
and the lapwing's winter cry
drawn from the farmer robbed of his fields
drawn from the tribes driven into exile
drawn from a saw cutting bone

It is a sound distilled
from the edge of extinction
from war's obliteration
from the driving out of mercy.

It is sound that grinds against the skin
that lacerates the heart
but is not heard by all and so it must be amplified
a threnody for the loss of hope
played by the last surviving piper.

At the Storm's Edge – Frank McMahon

At the storm's edge
always, never knowing if it will discharge
and overwhelm, or if it will relent,
recede as the season drags itself upstairs and round the cot.
Or the days may reverse to the moment sundered
between joy and shock, the seconds scattered
across the antiseptic floor, silence drowning
the other's cry.
                Light aches on the newborn's face
in the muffled house. A ghost demands
its feed, forever probing at the teat
with blue, waxed lips, growing thin on dreams.
At the storm's edge there is always a prayer.

The ghost is clothed, in a shoe-box laid,
carried away, an exit to be registered.

THE INVISIBLE PLIGHT

It is not unusual to believe in justice and equality without making an effort to discover if people are being treated fairly. Sometimes the painfully accurate observations of poets and other writers are a wake-up call to what's really happening around us.

Hidden Homeless – Mike Harwood

Hidden homeless, the invisible plight:
not seen in hard rain-battered doorways
of high-end, high street luxury stores,
or urine-stained stairwells of city car parks.
For many live in less visible locations.
Hidden homeless, unseen, out of sight,
in garages, wastelands, cold caravans.
Some gain night shelter but many surf sofas.
The vulnerable young, where are their rights?

Hidden homeless, the invisible plight.
We see polystyrene cups held up in our streets,
but are sofas better than floors, floors better than pavements?
No room of one's own, clothes out of boxes;
other people's washing up in shared small kitchens.
Real change, not pity, where are their rights?
The right not to pretend there is nothing wrong.
The right not to outstay a friend's support.
The right not to fear running out of an option.

Hidden from help, the invisible plight.
The shock of the drop through the benefits gap,
trapped in a tent, confined to a cramped car at night.
Mother and family in temporary accommodation,
cross town from the school where her children have friends;
cast into B&Bs eighteen miles away,
with infrequent buses to cover the distance.
Or if Mum is in work, jobs fitting round children,
a home out of reach to rent or to buy.

There but for the grace, go you and go I.
Rent rise, job loss, just one pay day away.
Seen or unseen the homelessness plight.
Real change not small change, where are their rights?

We the Un(pronoun)ceable – Sue Johns

Ourselves (past):		Themselves (present):
The community		The excluded
The space to play	For/Of	The gang-membered
The five a day		The stopped and searched
The dignity		The postcoded

Ours (intensive):		Theirs (possessive):
The first kisses		The controlled
The party dresses	For/Of	The medicated
The perfect sense		The bitch-slapped
The promises		The refuged

Ourselves (archaic):		Themselves (continuous):
Safety-net		Food Bank
Home-visit	For/Of	Regenerate
Benefit		Universally credit
Affordable rent		Evict

WE (all of the above) apply for/demand OUR
reinstatement

WE (the undersigned)

Sign Here
Iofnodi Yma
Signez Ici
Firma Aqui
Podpisz Tutaj
Wole Nibi
وقع هنا
یہاں سائن ان
在这里

A Driving Out – Irma Upex-Huggins

as if they are off
the spittle and daub and the scales
the sweet coffee suddenly is bitter
as if I, a nakedness in a new garden
show a corruption, a new temptation
that threaten twenty-three undefiled
seated at the foot of the cross
sitting in the blood of the lamb
gatekeepers, seeking their salvation
shut the gates to threats of immorality

the church meeting command repent
repent Babylon, repent or go from me
this night I cast you into the darkness
go wander the blackness of your soul

a corruption of earth passed from me
and I entered a new heaven
for salvation too is mine.

In this age of invention – Ian Woolf

We have bread for the hundreds
and food for the thousands
water for the millions
till the rivers run dry.
But spare now a thought
for the Poor Interloper
who for the best of intentions
is left high and dry.

He may be down on the Embankment
or under the bridges
in the all-night café
or sleeping under the sky.
Life gave him a chance
but now he knows he's lost it
the dice when he tossed it
only stopped to roll by.

Is he just a meths drinker
or a deep social thinker
condemned by his impecunity
and the ravages of time?
When from the world there's no greeting
we're all off to a meeting
our coffers are full
and we don't have a dime.

Would the price of a cuppa
really set your heart racing
or to keep out the cold
a glass of mulled wine?
In this age of invention
do you have water retention
when your eyes are so red
and your cheeks they don't shine?

In this age of invention
are you seeking redemption
or from high up in Heaven
a mark or a sign?
But the bridge now he's crossed it
and the count now he's lost it
still wait for me and you
and the passage of time.

Winter Hemispheres and Summer Latitudes – Sunita Thind

'You are addicted to yourself and how you feel every fucking second of the day' Burnt film

I remember summer latitudes
Filleted bliss.
Sleek giants of marbled intoxicants.
The durations of infantile sweetness.
The dimpled summered joys.
Inhaling indispensable truffles.
Radiant joys gallop around my head.
I was merry and sun-burnt.
Groves of delight.
Shady and cloud white free
Winter hemispheres – dying in vain.
Ogre of heat and pressure.
I am no longer sucking the icing sugar of sticking fingers.
Emulsify me in this remarkable poison.
Fingering the final verdict.
Did I fuck up again?
The ingénue of intoxication.
I am illustrious and grim faced.
Would arsenic cultivate my end?
My cranium is contaminated by my many offences.
Carbon-based and rudimentary.
Bleach me.
Thawing the defacement of me.
Smudging my self-loathing.
I am burnt like a beast.

Birds 1 – Jane Sherwin

Along the terraced roof-tops the birds are gathering
It is a primal instinct to gather and migrate
when weather is contrary,
when food is scarce,
when danger threatens the life of the tribe.

Across our world the poor trek;
fear, hope and desperation all drive them,
their destination the Shangri-la,
the far side of the next mountain,
the next stretch of water.

Unlike the birds they carry baggage;
children too young to take wing on their own,
the old and sick, who do not simply die under the hedgerows,
the prejudices that will fire anew
distrust and enmity in new generations.

The politicians pronounce and fulminate
in International Fora,
humanitarian workers solicit charity and aid,
the person on the Clapham omnibus
feels a pang of pity.

Today's rubbish-bins are cluttered
with yesterday's newspapers.

Save The Children – Jane Sherwin

He sleeps on the floor of Dhaka's train station
on a double-page spread of the Bangladesh Times,
Discarded, once read, by Haris Kermodi,
as he left for his office, to wheel and to deal.
The rest of the paper is being used too:
a batch of small children asleep in the dust.

What do they dream of?
Faraway families where they were loved?
Faraway families where they were beaten?
Parents who died? Mothers in childbirth,
fathers in accidents, working all hours,
taking short-cuts that ended in tragedy?

Maybe the sun and the shade of the trees
now left behind. The song of the birds,
the kiss of the breeze. The odour of curry:
the feel of a belly that's satisfied, full.
Maybe a future where they will be happy,
sleep in the warm, get work and earn money.

Haris Kermodi, discarding his paper,
bought fresh every day, gives never a thought
to the fate of these children on Dhaka's train station,
in Mumbai, Kolkata…
Lives of no value, like yesterday's paper,
lives that are taken by rapists and traffickers.

Yesterday's paper, crumpled and useless,
thrown down in the gutter
or blown by the wind…
the wind has no name,
no history, future…
nor have those children in Dhaka's train station.

Darkness versus Lightness – Martin Brummitt

We grow accustomed to our misfortunes
Darkness descends and we're trapped within a maze of our own
making
And the only way out is to find a sign or, failing that,
Hope a star comes out within
And that lightness reappears.

Padlocks – David Punter

The railings are covered in padlocks.
They sweat and glint in the heat,
And their messages are incomprehensible
Like gothic graffiti on high buildings
Or under sombre railway arches.

They seem to say, 'I will return,'
Or perhaps, 'We have drowned,'
Under this endless bridge, Rialto,
Waterloo, Golden Gate; we leave this
As a signature, a bond, washed-up debris.

Lock and key, ball and chain, the present
Wells around us; across this bridge
Come the refugees, the immigrants
Selling fake handbags, cheap umbrellas,
Jewels the colour of another starlit night.

The padlocks make a sound, a tiny
Tinnitus, making the bridge sway.
What is under the bridge, mummy –
Will the dark waters eat me?
The padlocks show rust the colour of gold.

English Lessons – Tim Waller

Each day we work on reading, sentence structure,
pronunciation, tense of verbs and vocab

appoint   appointed   appointment

Thank you, he whispers before we continue
to practice, sharing a coffee

sweet   sweeter   sweetest

Google for news about Canada, refugee camps,
immigrants, jobs

hope   hoped   hoping

admission to a university -
a solution for a visa extension.

dream   dreaming   dreams

Playing Monopoly, I tell him again how clever he is
passing go, collecting $200, saving a free get out of jail card.

smart   smarter   smartest

With so many hotels, you're really smart, I say.
I'll never forget this life, he says. *Thank you.*

A Day at a Park in Early Spring – Tim Waller

From a stadium barely visible, a crowd roars -
encouragement for a favorite team.

Families stroll toward a carousel, bumper cars,
the smell of popcorn hangs heavy.

A white-haired man walks a black dog.
Both stop to listen to us practice English.

He smiles when you mispronounce refugee.
Then gives the A-Okay signal when you get it right.

I wonder if you will come to this park after I leave.
Perhaps to write your mother a letter about your
                                        chances for Canada.

On the way home we buy white tulips.
I make plans to extend my ticket.

At the Hard Rock Café, you eat your first cheeseburger.
I'm no longer afraid to say, *I love you.*

PLANETARY BLUES

The latest UN research on Global Warming suggests we are no more than 12 years from a "tipping point" – when damage to the planet's ecosystems will accelerate beyond humanity's ability to repair. Already, climate refugees and endangered species are paying the price for thoughtless use of resources. Many poems in this section imagine what the world will feel like if governments and big corporations fail to cooperate effectively to avert climate catastrophe.

Global Warming Comes to the Allotment –
George Wright

The clay is baked hard
And even the stamping boot
Struggles to break the clods
Created with such abandon
In the soaked-soil spring

Gleaming white roots
Of bindweed, fibres of couch grass
Smile back at the fork
From concrete fortresses
Of enfolding invulnerability

And the gardener ponders
On recipes that might cure
Bruised heels or sore insteps
Whilst soothing a parched throat
With swigs of sun-warmed Stella

Whilst that other celestial object
Beats down with all her fury
Through the Factor Fifty Sunblock
Which is -anyway- washed away
With the sweat of exertion

Then the midges arrive
For their salty feast
Whilst the gardener's triumph
Of the odd crushed boulder
Settles dust in all his orifices

Several weeks of this
Can create some useful reflections,
Such as, how dare we
Criticise those farmers
Who grow food in dry climates?

The Arctic Circle – Belinda Singleton

The Arctic Circle shudders in its sleep:
The ice cracks up. No joke's intended there.
It's time to wake, or let our children weep.

The time is now, with promises to keep.
Galapagos has plastic waste to spare.
The Arctic Circle shudders in its sleep.

You'd think that action plans run far and deep –
not indolence, denial and despair.
It's time to wake, or let our children weep.

Some scientists advise a planet leap
away from sinking ships and stinking air.
The Arctic Circle shudders in its sleep.

The way is hard, the cost is sharp and steep:
how steep with global powers so late to care?
It's time to wake, or let our children weep.

Right now small islands drown as floodlines creep.
Across the ice a hopscotch polar bear.
The Arctic Circle shudders in its sleep.
Unless we wake, there'll be no child to weep.

Ice – Patric Cunnane

You're gonna make us lonesome when you go
Scared and warmer than we want
Penguins, seals and polar bears go first
Left without a rink

Won't be long before you're water
We can't splash our way out
As waves sweep everything away
And we swim over chimney tops

Breasting shoals of cartons
Escaped from old McDonald
We can't rattle you in our Scotch
Pack peas and TV dinners in your embrace

A million distractions
Kept us sleepwalking through the years
Deaf to the sound of you cracking up
Too late now, too late for our tears

Lilieth Leapt the Electric Fence – Pete Murry

Lilieth leapt the electric fence,
Maybe, at the time, it made sense,
To pounce, claws extended, at a bird in flight,
And so, fall into freedom by accident.
Or maybe she made a deliberate jailbreak,
'cause you gotta do what you gotta do,
To get outta the zoo.
Who knows what a lynx thinks?

But briefly, Lilieth the lynx got away
And was no longer on display,
She was no longer confined,
To be admired or to be ignored ,
By the curious, the awestruck, or the bored.
Peering through the wire.

Perhaps real freedom then kicked in,
With no food and drink provided,
Out in the woods and the fields and hills,
To eat she has to hunt and kill,
And at first maybe she has an edge,
As it must be centuries,
Since any lynx walked and stalked
Along these thickets and hedges,
So maybe some rabbits and mice,
Or a bird or two, turned just too late
And drew their last breaths,
Between the jaws of golden-eyed death.

Sadly, hunters can be hunted too,
And Lilieth could not be left to be free,
She was the 'property' of a zoo,
And large predators in Britain just cannot be,
Unless they're members of the bourgeoisie.

Uncaught Lilieth caused official fear
Alleged to pose a risk "severe",
So a killing bullet, not a tranquilising dart,
Was sent to stop this beauty's heart.

But the wheel will turn, and justice will be done,
And free once more, Lilieth will run,
Padding along on larger paws,
With longer, stronger, deadlier claws,
Reborn a larger, fiercer cat,

She'll rip out the throats of bureaucrats.

Altitude – Rebecca Gethin

Let's say that no-one implanted DNA
from the last Pyrenean Ibex into a goat
and its de-extinction lasted seven minutes.

Let's say the tree falling in the storm missed
that last *bucardo* (named Celia)
and she clattered away over the rocks on her Ninja hooves,

skipping across almost vertical scree to the herd where
youngsters frolic-jumped in the snow and her mate,
with his weighty swoop of horns, mane long and thick,

fur the colour of stones, stood like a boulder on the edge
of a precipice he walked up and down. Let's say he was
                                        never shot –
such an easy target in his stillness, those horns a trophy;

that their altitudes were never colonised by goats and sheep,
that migrations nourished them in all seasons,
that thick-furred winters and rock-hot summers were
                                        all still possible.

The Apple and the Pear – David Punter

As water levels rise and islands sink,
As wars are fought for gain of profiteers,
As powers ascend and smaller peoples shrink,
So the apple and the pear cannot shed tears.

As children die in cities scorched by fire,
As suffering mothers moan for swift release,
As presidents are ruled by guns for hire,
So the apple and the pear cannot bring peace.

As words lose meaning, and the post-truths reign,
As the light fades from history's telescope,
As all things bow to an artificial brain,
The apple and the pear cannot bring hope.

For all the humble, in their night of dread,
For all the poor, despised, ignored, controlled,
For all the mouths still waiting to be fed,
The apple and the pear are growing cold.

Part III from The Fourth Episode – David Kuhrt

The city dweller arrives at the seaside
thirsting for a horizon. He isn't in luck:
No-one can drink salt water.

Why take a holiday? He isn't a gypsy.
A Gypsy abhors settlement and is easily moved.
He is the salt of the earth.

He comes into town
as the citizen dies of thirst. His family
hires a gypsy to play music.

At the funeral, the eyes of the family
are filled with tears. At last
they have seen the horizon.

Gypsies have been here before. In cities
a horizon is a dotted line; a fence
punctuated by tears.

People squeeze through the gaps
and get stuck. Gypsies offer to help.
They are kicked out of town.

The reason for this is security:
Unauthorised access through fences
makes them fall down.

People are beginning to move. There is salt
in the air. You can see the horizon.
Why are we still here?

Global Warming is not just another good summer – Sue Johns

Whole communities have been destroyed we've all seen the footage. Everyone knows that if you are left hot you will stink – odours can be persuasive but most desires can be quenched with the stagnant water from dead flowers. Of course, they're wild they've been hacked with a pair of scissors and labelled with a life span. Why? Out of whimsy. How often? When they're under ten quid a bunch. But at least there are no axes involved and besides there is always plenty of dead wood to set light to. One cure for burning-up is to eat the flames and swallow the darkness, not like a self-immolating monk more like a circus act. As it is, with the worms, the rain needs a little bit of everyone. The sunshine is all too predictable, the rain, when it comes, it just comes – like the first and final fuck.

You and the Storms – George Wright

For you, the wing-footed God tumbles
The mercury has fallen and you know,
Or do not know, any more than the barometer,
When the mountains grow above your head;
Though enough for you to stir, to put down the book,
To look out and up from the locked casement
At the bird-throwing sky.

You capture reflection on the wind's swift journey
From 'high' to 'low,' in its gush to fill the quiet centre,
Where movement itself unites with the tick-tock
                              of the clock.
You know the unseen streams of their momentum
To the top of the globe; across the bridge to the turbulence
That reaches your own inner core, where both are
Beyond any divination.

There can be neither mastery, nor foresight, nor
Any alteration to the changes that are due to come;
No devices or technologies possible to affect
That which is due or that which has blown past and
The debris of our broken meteorology will not stand
The shattering wind or its inexorable increase, there can be
Only a battening down.

So, when all else fails, draw the drapes over
                              ever-inking skies,
Flame up the candles in the protection of jars
To inure their flickers from probing draughts,
Where the screaming winds defy any un-caulked space.
This is all we have against storms.
The only knowledge we can apply from
Life in the turbulent zone.

Storm Warning – Gillian Petrie

.... I tell them
who are standing in the field at dusk
as wind gets up
I say to them
who look at me with hostile eyes
I plead with them as thunder cracks
and rain smites down
and blanks the moon
they look at me with hollow eyes
and turn their backs
and march in line between the dunes
not breaking step
along the track
across the spit
towards the wreck
and out to sea.

pressure dropping
ocean rising
happening
now.

Tree – Tina Morris

They didn't tell us
what it would be like
without trees.

Nobody imagined
that the whispering of leaves
would grow silent
or the vibrant jade of spring
pale to grey death.

And now we pile
rubbish on rubbish
in this dusty landscape
struggling to create
a tree

but though the shape is right
and the nailed branches
lean upon the wind
and plastic leaves lend colour
to the twigs

we wait in vain for the slow unfurling of buds
and no amount of loving
can stir our weary tree
to singing.

A Hum of Green

A much-needed impetus in protecting our world, its peoples and other, increasingly endangered, species, is recognising and celebrating the beauty of Nature— poems on which subject occupy this last section.

Bearer of the Spark – Michael Tanner

Winter has come
And we wait for
the Tinder Box Man
With his staff
And his dusty coat
His moss-trimmed hat
His cat, his sack, his tin.
And his faraway eyes.

Some will invite him in
For a cup of ale
And a crust
But always he stays outside.
With his sack, his cat
And his cord-dangled rusty tin
He knows better than to come in.

He smells of the beech
And the oak,
Of fungus
Of smoke
That sleeps in his box
Though in his eyes
Is the tiniest spark,
A kind of surprise
From one in so shabby a guise.

Winter is here
Without words
The birds and the forest know
No need to wait for the wind
And the snow
Yet none in the village know
Where the Tinder Box Man will go
With his cat, his tin and his staff –
To sit by what hearth.

Snails at Saint-Michel-en-Grève – Michael Tanner

Whiter than pearls
But lustreless,
Along this wind-dried
Salt-dried, thirsty shore,
Like necklaces
The snails are stitched to edge
Of leaf and stem
Of thistle, fennel
Sea lavender –
Plants that have learned
To draw their life
From zones deaf to the tide.

With weight of this strange fruit
Their dulled leaves droop,
Catching the last of evening's light,
Tempting the listless passer-by,
Or couples dreaming,
To stoop and wonder at the sight.

Glow-Worms – Michael Tanner

Rain, after drought,
Has washed the August sky.
Stars, in their flocks uncountable
Browse the huge bowl of heaven
Beyond the tumbling satellites
And planes striving to destinations.

Their healing reaches to the harvest field
Soothing the raked stubble,
The little creatures of this little earth.

On the moist margins of the road
Snails creep skywards;
The white Campion shows pale,
And there and there
Keeping a tryst,
You find another miracle:
A colony of pulsing gems
Wooing their sister stars
With constellations of more gentle fire.

Vultures – Pete Murry

In Spain at Monfrague
Three hundred vultures live on a crag.
I have seen them with my own eyes.
They have seen me and ignored me,
A fat man who gets out of a van and
Gapes up in awe.
Some sit on ledges,
Some perch on edges,
And let go, to fall,
Spread wings and soar.
They may circle and glide,
Find a thermal to ride
In spirals and gyres
Higher, higher and higher,
Silently curving, intersecting, interlacing
In a broad-feathered dance in the sky
Over the Tagus gorge
Over the valleys and woods,
Up ever into pure azure

High above apes with their words.

Gannets – Rebecca Gethin

On elbows of white wings
        dipped in jet
they ride along gulleys
of waves, rising
        over the crest
            as it topples,
beyond gravity –
aerial minesweepers
        with searchlight eyes.

On chimneys of updraft
they swirl round
        catch gusts on a slant
with tilted wings,
        flexing, tensing
        tightly reefed
knowing all the possibilities
        but easeful
as if they hunted
        with wind.

Spiralling higher
        they weapon their wings
bullet themselves into water,
        vanishing   one by one
in a blowhole of spray,

re-appear –

bottle on the surface   to swallow,
shake out their wings
        for the up and aloft.

From Part IV "for Yolick and all migrating birds" in the Second Episode – David Kuhrt

Before the window, we touch extremities,
the wonderment of dextrous hands, this underpraised
embodiment, and see how brambles frame casement
and sash to describe arcs, a rampant garden
half unreal but rainbowed. Tomorrow
we'll start with spades and turn catastrophe
to our advantage. The irrepressible rose still blooms.

In thickets like briar, clematis arcades
on fallen trellises and armies of irises wait,
flat in origami folds, to flower. Cats reconnoitre
between. Years-old wisteria, knotted to the eaves
is illuminated like the Book of Kells. We dwell
on recent head-lines. Share their disaster.
Trace within ourselves the ancestral tract of land.

A living poem about the tree which adopted me – Martin Brummitt

Completely still, quiet and passive
No almost still, but not quite
Whispering into life
it's as if a leaf starts moving
then the others follow its lead
I wonder why?
My mood is changing
A star has come out – within
I'm resetting the clock
Brightness replaces Darkness.
The colour of the leaves shimmering and
glimmering as the sun glides
and slides over them.
Still no sign of squirrels or birds
Stone the crows
I've just seen two Parakeets shoot out
from **my tree**.

Deep in the Wood – Jenny Messer

Walking early morning,
as the light comes up,
birdsong fills the air
my mind sings.

The wood beckons,
I stand among trees
tall and proud as Masai warriors.
Branches reach up
what is this life,
whose souls pass this way?

I think about those departed,
the lives and loves gone.
A woodpecker chips away
like a lover pecking at my heart.

Deeper into the wood
I walk with the Masai,
happy to have loved
and to be loved.

Blackbird Love – Muir Hunter

High up, among the treetops, we embrace,
Listening to the dawn blackbird.
His crystal notes resound in the growing light,
His music plays around our bodies,
Orchestrating our passions.

The bird proclaims:
                    This is my kingdom;
These are my boughs that I sing to defend,
Where we shall lay our eggs.
When you have flown away, and your nest is empty,
We shall still be here,
Singing, claiming our trees.

Cumbria – Christie Dickason

Surprise! You thought
you were there,
a casual pilgrim
pacing the familiar
surface of the earth
among roads, trees,
cafés, telephone wires,
all the usual props.

Suddenly, you slide down
the opening drop
of an unexpected valley to
another place
embraced by private
hills and traced
by hidden streams
where your heart
sits up, awake at last,
to pay attention.

Night Garden – Christie Dickason

Here. Now…
In a sense of falling:
fragrance of rose
a single leaf
hope and silence.

The beginning is now.

Listen…
Lives too small to risk the light
stir now.
A bending leaf, loud as a drum
The footfall of a moth
My breath, a gentle march.

Listen…

Small lives
uncurl, flower,
stir the darkness with their tiny cries
swim out into the vast fragrant blackness
of the night.

Listen…
It begins.
Listen…

Shimmer – Christie Dickason

A hum of green gently shakes
the earth awake. Small green knives
slice through winter's grip.
Snowdrops fill cold spaces in the soul.
'Here's light,' they murmur.
'Again, here's light!'

Excited insects creak and churr.
Unfurling songs now
rise and swell. Uncurling tongues
of yellow, and blue. Great chords
of greens - honeysuckle leaves,
pale beech, the nettles' silver teeth.
Primrose, woodruff, moschatel,
pink cuckoo flower, marsh marigold
The anthem swells - 'Speed well! Speed well!'

A radiant flinging-up of thorn
now shouts with joy. Blackbirds reply.
Larks stitch together earth and sky.
Ragged Robin sings, and meadow sweet,
Knapweed, sorrel, full-bellied sheep,
The shameless diapason soars.
'The light returns! Here's life!'

Now come the massed full-throated tones
of plump and honey-weighted may.
Braided waters drum on stones.
Can-can heifers kick the air
above unfurling garlic moons.

Eggs press at the hearts of laying hens.
Dogs writhe, feet up, in ecstasy.
The world agrees on flat-out bliss -
this renewed perfection of beginning,
another chance to get it right.
The light is here! At last, the light!

REFERENCE

Index of Authors

Author Biographies

Martin Brummitt worked in accountancy then travelled extensively around Europe and spent seven years in Spain teaching English. For a long while he was a carer for his brother and then his mother, which helped him develop resilience and empathy for the problems of others. Martin describes himself as an Accidental Poet. He has always enjoyed reading and poetry but, until recently, didn't feel he had the tools or confidence to write creatively. "They say men are from Mars and women from Venus but I'm from neither planet. If anywhere I'm from Pluto."

Kathleen Cornelia's writing explores the underbelly of life's quotidian moments and their tragic or unanticipated turns, Though she calls London home, her pieces carry the imprint of her life in America.

Patric Cunnane's latest collection, *The Ghost of Franz Kafka* is published by Palewell Press. He co-organises readings by Dodo Modern Poets in London and elsewhere in the UK and Ireland. Patric lives in Folkestone and also writes fiction and drama. patric.poet@zen.co.uk. Tel: 01303 243868, https://dodomodernpoets.wordpress.com.

Christie Dickason grew up in five countries across four continents and learned young how to figure out the unspoken rules that every culture has. She worked as a mentor of students from abroad for the Royal Literary Fund, a theatre director, choreographer and Drama Officer for the Arts Council before turning writer. Christie is a published poet but also has nine internationally-published novels, including two international best-sellers. Collaboration as lyricist with award-winning composer Cecilia McDowell led to an opera, a mini-opera, and a residency at four farms across Britain to celebrate the organic landscape and husbandry, commissioned by the Bournemouth Sinfonietta Choir and Respect Organics with the backing of the Soil Association, and performances at the Eisteddfod, the Royal

School of Music, and St John's, Smith Square. She has written *The New Theatre Workshops* for the Calouste Gulbenkian Foundation and the Arts Council of Great Britain; and served as the Arts Council advisor and assessor for the project. Fellow of the Royal Literary Fund.

Max Fishel was born Liverpool, 1951, to European Jewish parents. Lived in Norwich 1970–76, then London until the present day. Worked in NHS for 5 years, state education for 40 and is now "retired." Plays Irish instrumental music in regular South East London session. Likes heavy duty Dutch salt liquorice. Best definition of health ever heard: "Health is the ability to adapt to change." Tries to write performance poems/ pieces/ songs/ tunes. Does spots at open mic poetry events around London. In last job, motto was, "Inclusion is for Everyone." Tries to help make this happen whenever possible. A dad, a grandad. A partner. A human.

Rebecca Gethin has written five poetry publications and has been a Hawthornden Fellow. *Messages* was a winner in the Coast to Coast to Coast pamphlet competition. New writing appears in various magazines and anthologies. *Vanishings* is forthcoming from Palewell Press and she is to run a short course for Poetry School.

Mike Harwood was one of 'Three Essex Poets' at the Essex Poetry Festival in 2014; he has also appeared in a 'Poetry in Performance' event at the Essex Book Festival, alongside Simon Armitage, and has read at the Shakespeare & Co Bookshop in Paris. His poetry has been published in *Chimera* magazine and in anthologies, including: *Genius Floored* (*2009*); *KJV: Old Text – New Poetry* (*2011*); *So Too Have the Doves Gone – reflections on the themes of conflict* (*2014*) and *Towards the Light - poems of reconciliation* (2018). Mike, formerly a lecturer in creative writing at the University of Essex, has worked as a volunteer for the homeless charity Emmaus, and is a founder member of

Creating Change Colchester, a campaign group connecting arts and activism to social and political change.

Jack Houston is his partner's (slightly) less-glamourous assistant in the running of their two-child household. He also works in Hackney's public libraries where he holds a regular evening poetry workshop at Woodberry Down Library on the second Tuesday of every month. His work has appeared in *And Other Poems, Brittle Star, The Butcher's Dog, Interpreter's House, The Lake, London Grip, Magma, Stand* and a few others, and in the anthologies *Urban Myths and Legends, The Emma Press Anthology of Love, The Head That Wears the Crown* (Emma Press) and *The Result Is What You See Today* (The Poetry Business). He has had work shortlisted for the Keats-Shelley and Basil Bunting Prizes, commended in the Interpreter's House Competition and the Ware Poets Prize, and has taken 2nd place in the 2017 *Poetry London* Competition.

Muir Hunter read Classics at Christ Church, Oxford and, while a student, helped evacuate children from republican Spain during the Civil War. He studied law, becoming a Queen's Counsel, founding Britain's first neighbourhood law centre and acting as Amnesty Observer at the trials of prisoners of conscience. With his second wife, Gillian Petrie, Muir was a founder-director of the Polish Hospices Fund and a founding-trustee of Nairobi Hospice, Kenya. His poems come from this rich mix of classical studies, public service and a passion for Justice.

Sue Johns originates from Cornwall where she started writing and performing as a 'punk poet.' Her work has been published in numerous magazines, most recently *Poetry News, The Morning Star, Prole, Southbank Poetry* and *The Atlanta Review*. Publications include a collection *Tantrum* 1998 and a pamphlet *A Certain Age* 2003. Her collection *Hush* was published by Morgan's Eye Press, 2011 and a pamphlet *Rented* by Palewell Press, 2018. Recent projects include a pamphlet inspired by trains and starting an M.A in Writing Poetry.

David Kuhrt was born in 1940 and has been writing poetry since 1959. As well as having poems appear in periodicals, his book-length, blank-verse narrative poem, *The Episodes: A Secret History of the Cold War*, was self-published in 2008. David also writes essays on philosophy and translates poetry by Rilke, Villon and others.

Frank McMahon's professional career has been in Social Work. He has written several full-length plays of which "A Death in Flanders" was broadcast on local radio last year. A second play is in preparation. Frank is a published poet on-line, (Poet by Day, Riggwelter, Fly on the Wall, Morphrog, I am not a Silent Poet) and in print: (Cannon Poets, The Curlew, Brittlestar.) He has written short stories (one published) and a children's novel. Frank lives in Cirencester and is a member of a local writers' group.

Jenny Messer was born near the sea and now lives by the Thames, water being a source of inspiration. She was a Picture Researcher at the Radio Times and a photographer's agent. She began writing 14 years ago after a brain injury but has been an avid reader since childhood.

Tina Morris has had seven poetry collections published and co-authored one with T K Metcalf. Her creative-prose work, *The Visitors*, was published by Calder & Boyars in New Writers 7. Her writing has appeared in many anthologies including *Children of Albion* (Penguin), *Doves for the Seventies* (Corgi), *New British Poetry* (BB Bks), *Poetry for Peace* (Breakthru Publications), and *Anthology of Little Magazine Poets* (Asylum Publications).

Pete Murry: After an ill-judged attempt to become a colossal squid, P R Murry was a founder of Apples and Snakes, and has worked with Worthless Words, Ragged Trousered Cabaret, and Dodo Modern Poets. He has been an active Trades Unionist and is a Green Party activist. He has lulu'd one book *Son of the Glowing Nightsoil of the Concealed Emu.*

M. Sahr Nouwah was born June 15, 1984 in a remote village in Sierra Leone, and presently works in Papua New Guinea as a Child Protection and Nutrition Advocacy Coordinator. He is a descendant of the Mano River Union and considers himself "a child of three nations." Schooled in Guinea, Sierra Leone and Liberia, Sahr is reading Management and Sociology but remains engaged in fighting social injustice especially for the Mano River Basin, Africa, and the World as a whole. He challenges issues affecting women and children within modern society, contributing and building a generation of Africans who can move the continent forward. https://medium.com/@msahrnouwah

OYOKO is a spoken word poet and visual artist, whose work reflects on social conscience, spirituality, and her ancestry. The Ghanaian London-based artist explores issues like race, social injustices, womanhood, sexuality and identity, drawing her inspirations from FKA Twigs, Sevdaliza and Arca. She forges her own African narrative through poetry, spoken word, sound and imagery. OYOKO's first single named *UNMORALITY* is out now - a piece that reflects an individual's willpower to construe what justice really must be. The poem comes with an audio-visual installation.
Instagram: @oyokothe
Facebook: @Theoyoko

Gillian Petrie worked in cancer care and the hospice movement: as head of Marie Curie's national home nursing service; as a founder-trustee of Nairobi Hospice, Kenya and founder-director of the Polish Hospices Fund which organised training for Polish doctors. In the 1990s she joined Kick Start Poets of Salisbury, becoming chair in 2000-2002. Her work has been published in anthologies: *Bedford Square 2* edited by Sir Andrew Motion (John Murray, 2007), *A Luminous Man - Muir Hunter, recalled with love* (Palewell Press, 2013) and in *Starters,* the publications of Kick Start Poets of Salisbury from 1998 onwards. In 2018, her collection *Metamorphosis* was published by Palewell Press.

David Punter is a poet and academic. He has published six pamphlets of poetry: *China and Glass, Lost in the Supermarket, Asleep at the Wheel, Foreign Ministry, Selected Short Stories* and *Bristol: 21 Poems*. He has had poems published in a wide variety of magazines in the UK and abroad, including *PN Review, Encounter, Thames Poetry, Other Poetry* and *The Puckerbrush Review*. David has taught literature in England, Scotland, China and Hong Kong; his most recent post as Professor of Poetry at the University of Bristol. He regularly performs with a group of poets and jazz musicians called Echoes and Edges. His first pamphlet with a leading publisher, *Those Other Fields*, will be published by Palewell Press in 2020.

Jane Sherwin was born in 1934 on the island of St. Vincent in the British West Indies. However, most of her life has been spent in England, often near the sea and, since coming to London, near the river. As well as being an Actor on Stage, and TV, and in Film, she was the Central America Coordinator for the British Section of Amnesty International, a Holy Fool and a Refugee Coordinator. She has also worked with the Homeless. She gave her life over totally to poetry at the age of 73; besides remaining a devoted great-grandmother. Jane has published several poetry chapbooks and her first collection, *Grandmother's Patchwork,* will be published in 2019 by Palewell Press.

Belinda Singleton came back to writing poetry after working in strategic management. She now spends part of her poetry life in Guildford, where she Chairs the lively Wey Poets group, and part in London where she reads widely. Her first full collection, *Foxes Don't Wear Watches* (Lapwing), was published in 2017. Her pamphlet *Wavelengths*, jointly authored with Kathryn Southworth, was published in 2019 (Dempsey & Windle). This year she is also editing Wey Poets' second anthology of recent times, *Pathways*.

Michael Tanner is mystified by most of what he sees, which might explain his fondness for question marks. He seems most of his many years to have lived on the edge of towns but not by choice. His greatest satisfaction comes from contact with the natural world, particularly lonely places and from writing. He considers himself a fortunate man: having helped to raise two families, had a share of 'adventure,' having learned to write, and never having lived too far from blackbirds, foxes and the sea. Amongst his main interests are the phenomena of language and languages, the restoration of habitat to those creatures which have lost it, Russian music, and sustaining the vigorous use of his two legs. He was once a marathon runner. He writes articles for an environmental forum and tries to keep up with developments in ecological awareness. To-date he has had one novel published (The Fogou Episode) and many poems at a national level, by Macmillan Education, Country Life and in reputable poetry magazines and anthologies.

Sunita Thind: I have always been passionate about my writing and now I have the time to concentrate on it fully. I have dabbled in many things including being a model, primary and secondary school teacher and trained as a make-up artist. Make-up, poetry and animals are my passion. I have recently suffered from Ovarian Cancer and am grateful I have survived it, but I am not in remission yet. All these experiences have coloured me as a person and enriched the poetry I write. I love to sing and take singing lessons and have a beautiful, male Samoyed puppy named Ghost.

Irma Upex-Huggins refers to herself as a 'words sculptor.' She is a retired Mental Health Social Worker and Group Analytic Psychotherapist. She lives in Croydon with her husband and dog, Kiki. She describes herself as an 'inquisitive observer of people, looking in from outside.' She enjoys travelling, loves the intimacy of small places: island communities, small towns, always visiting markets on her travels and learning about people, lives, languages, customs. She is the author of three poetry books:

Aloes and Brown Sugar (1991), *Charcoal Woman* (1993) and *Red Winds* (pb Palewell Press 2018). Irma is a member of Poets Anonymous. She plays guitar.

Tim Waller, an American poet, has been published in London and the US. He has been successful in competitions, placing in the Barnet Competition and being listed in the Troubadour Prize (2018). He has performed his poetry at many venues, including Torriano, Fourth Friday, and the Dugdale. Further, he has read with the Dodo Modern Poets, and helped to raise money in a Poemathon for the Enfield sponsorship of two refugee families. In his spare time, he enjoys walks with friends along the Thames.

Margaret Whittock is a retired academic who now writes novels, short stories and, more recently, poetry. Having independently published three novels in varying genres, including Young Adult, Noir and Historical, she is currently working on a volume of ghost stories, set in Ireland, and a sequel to her historical novel, *Ghost of Gallipoli*. Further details of all the author's work can be found on her website: http://darkmournepress.com.

Ian Woolf studied languages at school and went on to travel extensively around Europe. Having started work in sales and marketing in the late 1960s, he was laid low with a bi-polar condition 30 years ago. He subsequently turned to teaching, playing Spanish classical guitar, and writing poetry and music; and has also spent time in farming and looking after animals.

George Wright was born in London in 1944. As a child, his annual family 'holiday' was spent on the hop-fields of Kent, giving him an abiding love of the countryside. He had a range of jobs: as a farm labourer when he lived in a tent in a field for a year; a builder's labourer; barrow-boy and a railway parcels clerk, before entering social work. He is married and has two daughters. He worked in Kent and Lancashire, specialising in mental health social work, and managed services for people with learning difficulties in Croydon. He worked for Southwark Council, in forensic social work, then for Unison as a full time Branch official. Now retired, his interests include voluntary work as a 'Reader Leader,' leading weekly poetry reading sessions for people with dementia. He is also the Secretary of his local Park Committee, has an allotment and is a member of Croydon Poets Anonymous.

Palewell Press

Palewell Press is an independent publisher handling poetry, fiction and non-fiction with a focus on books that foster Justice, Equality and Sustainability. The Editor can be reached on enquiries@palewellpress.co.uk

www.ingramcontent.com/pod-product-compliance
Lightning Source LLC
Chambersburg PA
CBHW060958050726
47592CB00003B/1260